My Friend Has Autism

by Amanda Doering Tourville

illustrated by Kristin Sorra

Thanks to our advisers for their expertise, research, and advice:

Samuel H. Zinner, M.D., Associate Professor of Pediatrics
University of Washington, Seattle

Terry Flaherty, Ph.D., Professor of English
Minnesota State University, Mankato

PICTURE WINDOW BOOKS
a capstone imprint

Editor: Jill Kalz
Designer: Nathan Gassman
Production Specialist: Jane Klenk
The illustrations in this book were created with mixed media – digital.

Picture Window Books
1710 Roe Crest Drive
North Mankato, MN 56003
877-845-8392
www.capstonepub.com

Library of Congress Cataloging-in-Publication Data
Tourville, Amanda Doering, 1980–
My friend has autism / by Amanda Doering Tourville ; illustrated by
Kristin Sorra.
p. cm. — (Friends with disabilities)
Includes index.
ISBN 978-1-4048-5750-6 (library binding)
ISBN 978-1-4048-6109-1 (paperback)
1. Autism in children—Juvenile literature. I. Sorra, Kristin, ill. II. Title.
RJ506.A9T68 2010
618.92'85882—dc22   2009035267

Printed in the United States of America in North Mankato, Minnesota.
042016
009710R

My name is Nick. This is my friend Zack. Zack and I belong to a model airplane club. Zack has autism.

Airplanes are awesome!
Zack likes building bi-wing planes.

Fighter jets are
my favorites.

DID YOU KNOW? Autism is a brain-based
disorder. With autism, parts of the brain don't
grow the way they should. No one knows why
some kids have autism. There is no cure yet.

5

Zack knows a lot about airplanes. His nickname is Pilot. I've learned more about planes from Zack than from anybody else.

Sometimes Zack goes on and on about airplanes.
He repeats the same facts over and over.

DID YOU KNOW?
Kids with autism have trouble communicating. They may not talk much at all. They may talk only about their interests, even when other people don't share those interests.

It can seem like he's in his own world.

When Zack is focused on his models, he may not talk to me at all.

DID YOU KNOW?
Many kids with autism are able to focus very tightly on an interest.

We work on our own planes quietly, or I'll tell him about my day. I feel like I can tell Zack anything.

11

Zack and I play video games while we wait for the glue to dry.

He's tough to beat!

Sometimes I think he lets me win.

Zack hears things most people don't notice. Loud noises can hurt his ears. On our field trip to the airport, he wore the coolest earmuffs ever. He looked like he worked there.

DID YOU KNOW? Many kids with autism may hear sounds or smell odors that other people don't notice.

I wrestle with some of my other friends but not with Zack. He feels things differently than most people.

Zack doesn't like anybody touching him—not even to pin on his new wings!
And that's OK.

There are lots of things
I don't like, too.

When **I** go to Zack's house, **I** bring my own models.
It bothers Zack when other people touch or play
with his models. Each plane has
to be in just the right spot.

DID YOU KNOW? Kids with autism often spend a lot of time arranging toys or objects. It can upset them when someone moves their things.

Zack may not look at me while I'm talking to him. Sometimes he walks away.

DID YOU KNOW? Many kids with autism can seem impolite. They don't understand that it's rude to walk away from someone who is talking to them.

I know Zack doesn't mean to hurt my feelings.
I just show him my new magazine some other time.

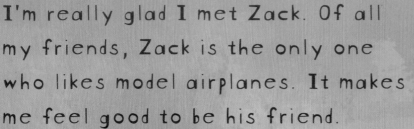

I'm really glad I met Zack. Of all my friends, Zack is the only one who likes model airplanes. It makes me feel good to be his friend.

I know that he likes being my friend, too.

What Is Autism?

Autism is a brain-based disorder. Doctors don't know what causes autism, and there is no cure. Kids with autism have trouble making sense of the world around them. They don't make connections with words and feelings like most people do. Kids with autism have trouble talking with others, which makes it hard to make friends. They often spend their time alone and seem to be "in their own world." Therapy can help kids with autism communicate with others and live better lives.

Glossary

arranging—putting things in order

communicating—sharing thoughts, feelings, or information

disorder—a kind of illness that affects the mind or body

impolite—not having good manners

therapy—treatment for an injury or physical or mental problem

upset—to bother or anger someone

To Learn More

More Books to Read

Robbins, Lynette. *How to Deal with Autism.* New York: PowerKids Press, 2010.

Shally, Celeste. *Since We're Friends.* Centerton, Ark.: Awaken Specialty Press, 2007.

Shapiro, Ouisie. *Autism and Me: Sibling Stories.* Morton Grove, Ill.: Albert Whitman, 2009.

Internet Sites

FactHound offers a safe, fun way to find Internet sites related to this book. All of the sites on FactHound have been researched by our staff.

Here's all you do:

Visit *www.facthound.com*

FactHound will fetch the best sites for you!

Index

Look for all of the books in the Friends with Disabilities series:

My Friend Has ADHD

My Friend Has Autism

My Friend Has Down Syndrome

My Friend Has Dyslexia